TRAVELING
GRACES

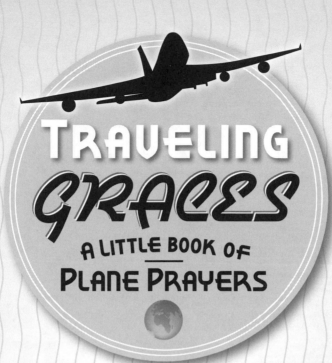

TRAVELING
GRACES
A LITTLE BOOK OF
PLANE PRAYERS

AGNES CUNNINGHAM, SSCM

Liguori
LIGUORI, MISSOURI

Imprimi Potest: Thomas D. Picton, C.Ss.R.
Provincial, Denver Province
The Redemptorists

Published by Liguori Publications
Liguori, Missouri 63057
To order, call 800-325-9521
www.liguori.org

Library of Congress Cataloging-in-Publication Data

Cunningham, Agnes, 1923-
    Traveling graces : a little book of plane prayers / Agnes Cunningham. — 1st ed.
      p. cm.
    ISBN 978-0-7648-1959-9
    1. Travelers—Prayers and devotions. 2. Air travel—Prayers and devotions. I. Title.
    BV283.T7C86 2010
    242'.88—dc22

2010018013

Liguori Publications, a nonprofit corporation, is an apostolate of the Redemptorists. To learn more about the Redemptorists, visit *Redemptorists.com.*

Printed in the United States of America
14 13 12 11 10   5 4 3 2 1
First edition

Acknowledgments

As I join the Liguori family, I must express my gratitude to Phoebe Collins, acquisitions editor, for her expertise, enthusiasm, and encouragement; to Christopher J. Miller, rights and permissions editor, for his professional responsibility, courtesy, and knowledge of all things necessary for publication; and to Brother Daniel Korn, C.Ss.R., for his interest, intuition, and initiative, without which, this project would still be somewhere in an airport hangar.

CONTENTS

PART II: SOARING

PART III: EARTHBOUND

DEDICATION

For Reverend John A. Jamnicky,
Chicago O'Hare International Airport [ORD]
1981-2000

THE AIRPORT CHAPLAIN

Lord,
This man has trained his eyes
    for depth (or height) perception.
    He has dreams that reach from here to
        extravagant hopes,
    a heart that, like your Father's house,
        has many mansions.

(Where else do they go—
    the airport homeless and the airport personnel;
    travelers lost, grief-stricken, lonely,
        with time to wait, or waste—
        when planes are cancelled or delayed?)

Lord,
The universe and all the spacious skies are yours.
Be yourself the airport chaplain's home:
    your eagle wings his strong support
    in low-ceiling weather,
    in solo-flight solitude.
Amen.

INTRODUCTION

CHECK-IN

March 19, 1960, marked the date of my first flight. We left Chicago under snow, ice and bitter cold, and arrived in Phoenix, where spring was at its loveliest.

Since that date, I have flown hundreds of thousands of miles, within the United States and Canada, and to more than twenty-five countries in Europe, South America, Africa and the Middle East.

My shortest flight was a helicopter hop from one airport (La Guardia) to another (Kennedy) to make a plane to Istanbul. My longest *unscheduled* flight was a four-and-a-half hour journey from Champaign, Illinois, to Chicago-O'Hare; tornado warnings, heavy air traffic, and the need to refuel lengthened, beyond imagining, what should have been a forty-minute trip.

Through all my travels, I have never ceased to re-experience my reactions to that first flight: the thrill of take-off and the certainty that every landing is a homecoming to new adventure.

The idea for this collection was born and evolved throughout my years of air travel. The opportunity to put it together in written form did not materialize until an automobile accident (and some broken bones) enforced a period of reduced activity, and provided the time necessary to begin this series of "flights of reflection."

AGNES CUNNINGHAM, SSCM

TRAVELING GRACES

Take-off

Lord,
Any moment now it will happen.
The plane will pick up speed,
    all motors racing,
    and we shall skim the surface of the runway
    to that zero point,
    where one great surge of energy
    will lift us up from solid earth,
    on still more solid air,
    to set us on our way.

Support us, strong and holy Lord,
    by your power and might.
Lift us on the everlasting wings
    of your loving providence.
Sustain us as we fly.
Hold us in your quiet, calming hands.
Enfold us in your gentle care.
Amen.

The next day John again was standing with two of his disciples, and as he watched Jesus walk by, he exclaimed, "Look, here is the Lamb of God!" The two disciples heard him say this, and they followed Jesus. When Jesus turned and saw them following, he said to them, "What are you looking for?" They said to him, "Rabbi" (which translated means Teacher), "where are you staying?" He said to them, "Come and see." They came and saw where he was staying, and they remained with him that day. It was about four o'clock in the afternoon.

JOHN 1:35-39

FIRST FLIGHT

Lord,
It scarcely seems possible
    that in this day of space shuttles
    and orbiting astronauts,
    I am flying for the very first time.

But, there you have it—
    as if I had to tell you!

Yes, I am jittery, excited,
    apprehensive,
    very much a pioneer of sorts,
    among all these others
    who look as if they do this every other day.

Thank you, surprising Lord,
    for this new experience.
    I want to be relaxed enough to live
        the fullness of this moment,
        exhilarated enough to make every
           bit of it my own.

Be with me, Lord of the skyways, with your blessing,
    as you have been present
    to every other first time
    in my life!
Amen.

Then Jesus called the twelve together and gave them power and authority over all demons and to cure diseases, and he sent them out to proclaim the kingdom of God and to heal. They departed and went through the villages, bringing the good news and curing diseases everywhere.

LUKE 9:1-2, 6

In The Cockpit

Lord,
    I caught a glimpse
        of the captain and the crew
        of this ship,
    as I passed the cockpit.

They looked competent enough,
    appropriately serious,
        but not glum,
    reassuringly at ease, and
    seemingly in control.

Lord of the airways
    that envelop this world
    and the great expanses of space,
    steady the hands,
    clear the minds,
    sharpen the eyes
    of those who guide our journey.

Ease their hearts of personal care,
    protect the friends and family
        they have left behind.

Keep them alert and far from
    boredom as they sit, masterfully,
    before that instrument panel
    in the cockpit.
Amen.

Therefore I prayed, and understanding was given me;
I called on God, and the spirit of wisdom came to me….
I loved her more than health and beauty,
and I chose to have her rather than light,
because her radiance never ceases….
For both we and our words are in his hand,
as are all understanding and skill in crafts….
The cycles of the year and the constellations of the stars…,
for wisdom, the fashioner of all things, taught me.

WISDOM 7:7, 10, 16, 19, 22

FLIGHT ATTENDANTS

Lord,
     These young men and women,
        who welcome us aboard,
     always intrigue me.

     In a sense, they are all
        of the same mold,
        graduates of the same flight attendant school.

     Yet, each one stands uniquely alone.

     Below the certified surface,
        the differences lie,
        ready to break through,
        given the least encouragement.

     Each one carries a story and a dream
        in a very human heart.

Lord,
     you came to us as a servant,
        in graciousness and compassion;
        you taught us to aspire
          to noble, lofty ideals.

Be with these men and women now, Lord,
    as they answer our demands
    and meet our needs.

Teach them to lift
    their hearts and minds
    in praise to you,
    as they walk and minister
    above the earth.
Amen.

Now there are varieties of gifts, but the same Spirit; and there are varieties of services, but the same Lord; and there are varieties of activities, but it is the same God who activates all of them in everyone. To each is given the manifestation of the Spirit for the common good....All these are activated by one and the same Spirit, who allots to each one individually just as the Spirit chooses.

1 COR. 12:4-7, 11

COMPANIONS IN FLIGHT

Lord,
    we've been in the air long enough
        for me to have had time
        to look around
        at all the others in this plane.

    I wonder where they've been
        and what their destination is.

    Are there any who have
        never known you?
    any who have walked away
        from your friendship?
    any you would call to a life
        of closer association with you
        and greater service of the poor and needy?

Reader of hearts and minds,
    Lord of the secret places of our lives,
    be close to my companions
        on this flight.

    Open their ears to the
        sound of your voice;
        their eyes,
        to the beauty of your face;

their minds,
   to the truth that you are;
their hearts,
   to your gentle, insistent love.

   Touch them, Lord, and quicken them to
      a new and blessed life.
Amen.

How very good and pleasant it is
   when kindred live together in unity!
It is like the precious oil on the head,
   running down upon the beard,
on the beard of Aaron,
   running down over the collar of his robes.
It is like the dew of Hermon,
   which falls on the mountains of Zion.
For there the LORD ordained his blessing,
   life forevermore.

PSALM 133

Flight Commuter

Lord,
Here we go again, you and me:
another day, another flight.

I step onto this carrier
    as if I were walking down a corridor
        between two offices.
In a sense, this plane
    has become a corridor
        linking home and work;
        bonding points of activity in my life;
        bridging the space between one project
          and the next.

Lord of the humdrum and the daily,
    renew my energies;
    give me new zest for living;
    enliven my enthusiasm
        for tasks, assignments, enterprises, jobs;
    give me fresh eyes to behold the wonders
        of your creative love —
    where I begin and where I end,
    and on this flight.
Amen.

"Pray then in this way:
Our Father in heaven,
hallowed be your name.
Your kingdom come.
Your will be done,
on earth as it is in heaven.
Give us this day our daily bread.
And forgive us our debts,
as we also have forgiven
our debtors.
And do not bring us
to the time of trial,
but rescue us
from the evil one."

MATTHEW 6:9-13

Morning Shuttle

Lord,
the morning has barely begun,
    and I've lived half-a-day already.

These early shuttle flights
    call for a rising hour
        I can't appreciate;
    they get me on the road
        before I'm ready;
    they have me seat-assigned
        too soon.

Perhaps I'll close my eyes,
    sleep again—
    let breakfast pass me by—
    and wake to a new day
        in an hour or so.

Be patient with me, Lord,
    and remember that you slept once
    in a little boat
        on the Sea of Galilee.
Amen.

My heart is steadfast, O God, my heart is steadfast.
I will sing and make melody.
Awake, my soul!
Awake, O harp and lyre!
I will awake the dawn.
I will give thanks to you, O LORD, among the peoples,
and I will sing praises to you among the nations.
For your steadfast love is higher than the heavens,
and your faithfulness reaches to the clouds.

PSALM 108:1-4

Carry-on Luggage

Lord,
try as I might,
>it seems I always have to take along
>>more than I intend,
>and return with more than I take:
>clothes to wear,
>papers to read,
>souvenirs,
>unfinished business.

Not only is this baggage bothersome;
>but it takes up space
>>where my legs want to stretch out.
>It gets in the way,
>slows me down,
>needs to be remembered.

You told us, Lord,
>to give away the second cloak,
>to travel without purse and staff,
>to sell all and give to the poor.

Teach me how to live with open hands,
to embrace the simple life, but always
to respect the goods that
your bounty sends as gift and blessing.

Help me to learn to travel,
unencumbered,
lightly,
quickly,
grace-fully.
Amen.

"Blessed are the poor in spirit, for theirs is the kingdom of heaven."

MATTHEW 5:3

"Do not store up for yourselves treasures on earth, where moth and rust consume and where thieves break in and steal; but store up for yourselves treasures in heaven, where neither moth nor rust consumes and where thieves do not break in and steal. For where your treasure is, there your heart will be also.

MATTHEW 6:19-21

CRUISING

Lord,
> I've forgotten
>> what the captain said
>> about our altitude,
> but we're cruising now.

> If I close my eyes,
>> I feel that we are standing still,
>> caught in a moment of
>> immutability,
>> suspended in some
>>> unknown dimension of place
>>> between two breaths.

> I want to pretend that
>> *just now*
> I've stepped beyond myself,
>> with all of myself,
>> on to infinity,
>> into eternity.

Lord of a love that your friends,
> the saints,
> have measured in
> "breadth and length and height and depth,"
> lead us into the everywhere
>> of your presence.

Let us "live and move
and have our being,"
inalterably,
in the will—your own—
that is our peace.
Amen.

O LORD, my heart is not lifted up,
   my eyes are not raised too high;
I do not occupy myself with things
   too great and too marvelous for me.
But I have calmed and quieted my soul,
   like a weaned child with its mother;
   my soul is like the weaned child that is with me.

PSALM 131:1-2

Meal Service

Lord,
> You, more than anyone else,
>> know the importance of a meal
>> for the nourishment of our bodies,
>>> minds, and hearts.

> You know that, as bread is broken,
>> friendships can be deepened;
>> as wine is shared,
>> relationships can be sealed.

> Even this silent partner next to me
>> has offered conversation
>> and the hesitating gestures
>> of a pleasant contact
>> with the arrival of our trays.

Bountiful, provident Lord,
> bless the food before us,
> bless us as we partake
>> of the fruit of the labor
>> of unknown, uncounted
>> men and women.

> You who feed the birds and clothe the lilies,
>> teach us to be grateful,
>> to hunger for imperishable food,
>> to thirst for living water.

Lead us more closely, every day,
    to the unity you will
    for those you have called together
        in one faith, one hope, one destiny.
Amen.

Now the Passover, the festival of the Jews, was near. When he looked up and saw a large crowd coming toward him, Jesus said to Philip, "Where are we to buy bread for these people to eat?... One of his disciples, Andrew, Simon Peter's brother, said to him, "There is a boy here who has five barley loaves and two fish. But what are they among so many people?" Jesus said, "Make the people sit down." Now there was a great deal of grass in the place; so they sat down, about five thousand in all. Then Jesus took the loaves, and when he had given thanks, he distributed them to those who were seated; so also the fish, as much as they wanted. When they were satisfied, he told his disciples, "Gather up the fragments left over, so that nothing may be lost." So they gathered them up, and from the fragments of the five barley loaves, left by those who had eaten, they filled twelve baskets.

JOHN 6:4-5, 8-13

TURBULENCE

Lord,
>No good pilot, I suppose,
>>misses all the air pockets.
>The seat belt sign is on,
>>and we're in for an uneasy time,
>>until this patch of wind and weather
>>is behind us.

>Strange that the flight reflects so well
>>the turmoil in my heart and mind today.
>There's still no peace for me
>>in the situation that absorbs
>>so much of my thought and feeling
>>and concern—my every waking moment.
>There's no escape from it.
>I live and breathe and, yes,
>>die, to some extent,
>>under the weight of restlessness and anguish.

Lord,
>You calmed stormy waves and anxious hearts
>>when you walked this earth;
>You drank the bitter cup
>>and lived to conquer death in all its forms.
>Grant me light to see a path through the confusion
>>in my life;

remember your promise and gift
of a peace beyond imagining.
Guide all the planes
that trace their way, this day,
along the unsettled roadways
of the skies.
Amen.

For God alone my soul waits in silence;
from him comes my salvation. He alone is my rock and
my salvation,
my fortress; I shall never be shaken....

For God alone my soul waits in silence,
for my hope is from him.
He alone is my rock and my salvation,
my fortress; I shall not be shaken.
On God rests my deliverance and my honor;
my mighty rock, my refuge is in God.

Trust in him at all times, O people;
pour out your heart before him; God is a refuge for us.

PSALM 62:1-2, 5-8

Jet Stream

Lord,
>I scarcely ever think about it
>>above the ground—
>the long trail of
>>signature,
>the wake of cloud and puff
>>behind an airship—
>that holds my eyes
>>when I look up from earth
>>to track another
>>climbing carrier.

Do others stand below
>to watch us now?
Does someone else catch sight
>of this plane's passing,
>and read the sign and message
>of our destination?

You know our need
>for signs and symbols,
>Lord.
>You came as the image
>of your Abba, Father.

You ask that we be testimony,
   a witness:
to speak your Good News,
to show forth your love,
to proclaim in word and action
      our faith in you
as Lord.
So be it.
Amen.

God said, "This is the sign of the covenant that I make between me and you and every living creature that is with you, for all future generations: I have set my bow in the clouds, and it shall be a sign of the covenant between me and the earth. When I bring clouds over the earth and the bow is seen in the clouds, I will remember my covenant that is between me and you and every living creature…. When the bow is in the clouds, I will see it and remember the everlasting covenant between God and every living creature of all flesh that is on the earth."

GENESIS 9: 12-16

Cloud World

Lord,
>I didn't think
>>we'd take off this morning.

>What a dark and dreary
>>day it was below!

>But, fly we did. And
>>what a sight
>>broke on our eyes,
>>as we came through
>>the rain and mist,
>>into the shattering sunlight
>>of a shining world above the clouds.

>They're all beneath us, now,
>>in wild and wonderful formation:
>>white and wispy, mountainous
>>and cotton-fluffed.

>We're floating through a land of
>>make-believe, it seems.

Lord of all lights,
>When I walk through
>>gray and foggy days,

Help me to remember
    that your sun is
    always shining above
    the ceiling,
    where clouds are never dark.
Amen.

And God said, "Let there be lights in the dome of the sky to separate the day from the night; and let them be for signs and for seasons and for days and years, and let them be lights in the dome of the sky to give light upon the earth." And it was so. God made the two great lights—the greater light to rule the day and the lesser light to rule the night—and the stars. God set them in the dome of the sky to give light upon the earth, to rule over the day and over the night, and to separate the light from the darkness. And God saw that it was good.

GENESIS 1:14-18

"GLORY"

Lord,
    all the conditions are right today:
    we're flying over soft, white,
        layer upon layer
        of seemingly unbroken clouds, and
    the sun is shining on our plane
        from the side across the aisle.

And there it is!

I see it through the window:
the small, but total shadow
    of this carrier,
    surrounded by,
    enclosed in,
the perfect circle of light
    that flyers call, "glory!"

The rainbow tints flash off
    as "glory" is reflected on cloud-vapor,
and we are borne along, it seems,
    by light, its very self.

Lord,
    All glory is yours.
    It shines out, in grandeur, as the poet said,
    "like shining from shook foil,"

and all the world is "charged"
    with the glory that is yours.

Bear us up, all the days of our lives,
    on eagle's wings,
    surrounded by light,
    embraced by love.
    Amen.

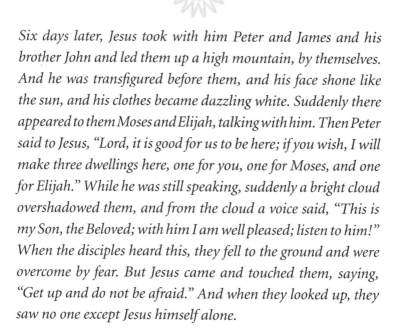

Six days later, Jesus took with him Peter and James and his brother John and led them up a high mountain, by themselves. And he was transfigured before them, and his face shone like the sun, and his clothes became dazzling white. Suddenly there appeared to them Moses and Elijah, talking with him. Then Peter said to Jesus, "Lord, it is good for us to be here; if you wish, I will make three dwellings here, one for you, one for Moses, and one for Elijah." While he was still speaking, suddenly a bright cloud overshadowed them, and from the cloud a voice said, "This is my Son, the Beloved; with him I am well pleased; listen to him!" When the disciples heard this, they fell to the ground and were overcome by fear. But Jesus came and touched them, saying, "Get up and do not be afraid." And when they looked up, they saw no one except Jesus himself alone.

MATTHEW 17: 1-8

Illusion

Lord,
    Somehow, I dozed,
        this trip—
    awakening to find
        great mounds of cotton balls,
        gigantic in size, surrounding us.

    The aircraft—fragile in cloud country—
        nosed its way, undaunted,
        as, above my head,
        a speaker blared:
        "Heavy cloud build-up over the lake…."

    Then, suddenly, all was blue below.
    We were, once again, free!

Lord,
    Wind, waves and clouds
        obey you, do your will.

    Let me not, alone of all your creatures,
        resist your word, your Word.
Amen.

A windstorm arose on the sea, so great that the boat was being swamped by the waves; but he was asleep. And they went and woke him up, saying, "Lord, save us! We are perishing!" And he said to them, "Why are you afraid, you of little faith?" Then he got up and rebuked the winds and the sea; and there was a dead calm. They were amazed, saying, "What sort of man is this, that even the winds and the sea obey him?"

MATTHEW 8: 24-27

Solitude in the Sky

Lord,
   more and more,
      I find myself looking forward
      to these flights
      as privileged times
      for thought and reflection.

   My days are filled from early to late
      with the business of life,
      and the busyness of living.

Here, in the sky,
   I find it possible—if I will—
   to enter another dimension of existence:
   to be alone
      without boredom or anguish;
   to look again
      at values and purposes;
   to re-examine the goals
      I pursue;
   to ponder;
   to pray.

Lord of the mountaintops and valleys
   of this universe,
   of desert places, and
   of all the secret corners of our hearts,

teach me the meaning and the
wealth of solitude,
that all my life may be
filled with your Spirit.
Amen.

As a deer longs for flowing streams,
so my soul longs for you, O God.
My soul thirsts for God,
for the living God.

PSALM 42:1-2

"And whenever you pray, do not be like the hypocrites;
for they love to stand and pray in the synagogues
and at the street corners, so that they may be seen by
others….But whenever you pray, go into your room and
shut the door and pray to your Father who is in secret;
and your Father who sees in secret will reward you.

MATTHEW 6:5-6

WEST INTO THE SUNSET

Lord,
>this is the most extraordinary day!

>How was I to know
>>that flying west at sunset
>>would be like this?

>I've been in the air almost an hour, now,
>>and I've just realized
>>that the sun hasn't dimmed one bit.

>In fact, it seems to be always
>>at the same point of splendor,
>>at the same peak of brilliance,
>>changing only to increase
>>>the range of its colors,
>>>the intensity of its existence.

>I'm going to sit back and enjoy
>>this three-hour sunset
>>and never again envy
>>Exupéry's Little Prince!*

Lord,
>You are light!
>Only in your light, can we see light.

*Antoine de Saint-Exupéry's *The Little Prince* describes a planet where one day he saw 43 sunsets.

Grant that my eyes be open to
    the beauty of your face,
    reflected in the features of those
    whom you call your friends.
Amen.

O LORD God of hosts, hear my prayer;
    give ear, O God of Jacob!
Behold our shield, O God;
    look on the face of your anointed.
For a day in your courts is better
    than a thousand elsewhere.
I would rather be a doorkeeper in the house of my God
    than live in the tents of wickedness.
For the LORD God is a sun and shield;
    he bestows favor and honor.
No good thing does the LORD withhold
    from those who walk uprightly.
O LORD of hosts,
    happy is everyone who trusts in you.

PSALM 84:8-12

STRETCH JET

Lord,
    Why do I always
        end up in the middle seat
        of a stretch jet
        just when I need it least of all?

    After a day of sitting in one chair,
        while covering the length and breadth
        of a mind-boggling agenda,
        my body has gone on strike.

    There's too much of it — of body, I mean —
        it hardly fits inside my skin;
        arms, legs, and all
        want to break out, run, jump
        or simply have room to be
            more comfortable.
  It's even too weary to let me
        fall asleep and forget it.

Lord,
    You have formed and fashioned us,
        knit bones together marvelously.
    You know the limits of our humanity,
        our earthiness, our finitude.

Help me to remember, today,
   your promise of a new and risen life,
      when this mortal flesh
      will put on immortality,
      and this all too restless heart of mine
      will find its rest in you.
Amen.

O LORD, you have searched me and known me.
You know when I sit down and when I rise up;
   you discern my thoughts from far away.
You search out my path and my lying down,
   and are acquainted with all my ways….
For it was you who formed my inward parts;
   You knit me together in my mother's womb.
I praise you, for I am fearfully and wonderfully made.
   Wonderful are your works….

PSALM 139: 1-2, 13-14

CAPACITY FLIGHT

Lord,
    Inflation and the cost of fuel,
        I know,
        are factors in the cut-back policies
        of fewer flights and fuller planes.

    When every seat is taken, though,
        it seems that breathing space
        is cut back, too…
  as if the over-population of our earth
        has reached into the skies.

    Perhaps, the issue is not so much too many people
        in one place.
        If we are really honest,
        we will acknowledge that
  the luxury of space is
        claimed more and more
        by fewer and fewer of
        earth's inhabitants.

    Perhaps, after all, poverty is
        the lack of necessary space
        of one kind or another
        in a human life.

Lord, as you hold all times and seasons
   in your gentle hands,
   as you shelter us all
      beneath the boundless shadow
      of your wings,
   grant us the grace to treasure the
      hours and spaces that are ours,
      that none be lost.
Amen.

"The kingdom of heaven is like treasure hidden in a field, which someone found and hid; then in his joy he goes and sells all that he has and buys that field.

Again, the kingdom of heaven is like a merchant in search of fine pearls; on finding one pearl of great value, he went and sold all that he had and bought it."

MATTHEW 13:44-46

International Journey

Lord,
    We've settled in, now,
        for the long flight
        and the short night.

    There's scarcely time to ready
        body, heart, and mind
        for new scenes, new places—
        amid the flight attendants' rigid schedule
        to get us from here to there.

    I'd like to skip the "meal,"
        forget the in-flight film,
        erase the hours of cruising,
        so as to be wide awake
        and ready
        to catch the first bright signs
        of early morning splendor,
        that breaks
        where West meets East.

Lord of the universe,
        of all times and places,
        let me be at home with you
        wherever I go in this world,

until the sojourning
and the wandering
are done;
and I find my rest
in the new heavens
and the new earth
you have promised us.
Amen.

And he died for all, so that those who live might live no longer for themselves, but for him who died and was raised for them....So if anyone is in Christ, there is a new creation: everything old has passed away; see, everything has become new!...For our sake he made him to be sin who knew no sin, so that in him we might become the righteousness of God.

2 CORINTHIANS 5: 15, 17, 21

One in Christ

Lord,
>   it is Easter Tuesday;
>   but Orthodox pilgrims with whom I left Cairo
>   wear Holy Week black.

>   Crowded together, children and lunches on laps
>   (in a plane that lacks more than tray tables!),
>   they are silent and somber,
>   as heavy air in the cabin.

>   Later, in buses that labor
>   from Amman through the Dead Sea desert
>   to Jordan's Jerusalem,
>   I leave them to walk in the light of one risen,
>   while they make their way to Calvary

Lord,
>   we are a pilgrim people.
>   Grant us wisdom and strength
>   to walk in shadow or sunlight,
>   trusting in your promise
>   that life follows death
>   and your mercy eclipses our sins.
Amen.

Holy Father, protect them in your name that you have given me, so that they may be one, as we are one….I am not asking you to take them out of the world, but I ask you to protect them from the evil one….I ask not only on behalf of these, but also on behalf of those who will believe in me through their word, that they may all be one. As you, Father, are in me and I am in you, may they also be in us, so that the world may believe that you have sent me….I in them and you in me, that they may become completely one, so that the world may know that you have sent me and have loved them even as you have loved me.

JOHN 17:11, 15, 20-21, 23

Vacation Bound

Lord,
    At last!
    After weeks (or is it months?)
        of saving, planning, and waiting,
        vacation time is here!
    My holiday began
        as I stepped on board this plane.
    I know the sense of exultation,
        of excitement, of freedom, too well
        to think otherwise.
    Can all these others sense my enthusiasm?
    Are there some who share it, and
    who want to shout out loud, *"up, up and away?"*

Lord,
    you invited your friends,
        to go away and rest with you.
    You knew, yourself, the need
        to step aside from
        your Father's work
        to renew your spirit.
    Help me to find in this special time—
        of fun and frolic,
        of relaxation and refreshment—
    a restoration of my energies,
    a fresh perspective on the whole of life,

and some new wisdom about the way
I can find rest with you,
    from day to day,
    when vacation time is done.
Amen.

*Then I saw a new heaven and a new earth; for the
first heaven and the first earth had passed away, and
the sea was no more. And I saw the holy city, the new
Jerusalem, coming down out of heaven from God,
prepared as a bride adorned for her husband. And I
heard a loud voice from the throne saying,
"See, the home of God is among mortals.
He will dwell with them;
they will be his peoples,
    and God himself will be with them;
he will wipe every tear from their eyes.
    Death will be no more;
mourning and crying and pain will be no more,
for the first things have passed away."*

REVELATION 21:1-4

EARTHBOUND

STAND-BY

Lord,
    Not everyone made this flight.
    The only reason I am here
        is because someone else,
        for whatever reason,
        didn't show.

    I'm grateful to be on my way,
        even though I didn't
        get first class seating,
        on *this* stand-by ticket.

    The hardest thing, of course,
        is the uncertainty of knowing
        when I'll be called, or
        if I'll get "bumped"
        before the plane takes off.

    I think I'm learning to be
        less anxious,
        more free,
        more careful of the way
            I plan my time,
        more humble in my expectations.

Lord,
     Help me to remember
        that you are always
        standing by me in my every need,
        ever provident in your
           watchfulness and care.
        Grant that I live this small experience
           of poverty with gracious humor.
   Amen.

"When the Son of Man comes in his glory, and all the angels with him, then he will sit on the throne of his glory. All the nations will be gathered before him, and he will separate people one from another as a shepherd separates the sheep from the goats.…Then the king will say to those at his right hand, 'Come, you that are blessed by my Father, inherit the kingdom prepared for you from the foundation of the world; for I was hungry and you gave me food, I was thirsty and you gave me something to drink, I was a stranger and you welcomed me, I was naked and you gave me clothing, I was sick and you took care of me, I was in prison and you visited me.' …And the king will answer them, 'Truly I tell you, just as you did it to one of the least of these who are members of my family, you did it to me.'"

MATTHEW 25: 31-32, 34-36, 40

CANCELLED!

Lord,
 I should have known it would happen.
 The weather has been too unpredictable,
  here and there:
  where I begin and
  where I want to go.

They've made some promises—
  the airline personnel,
  harassed, blameless,
  intent on preserving a
  carefully-constructed image
  that only adds to the tension.

Arrangements will be made:
  if not today, tomorrow.
For the moment, expectation supplants
  patience.
We investigate, explore the airport,
  seeking distractions, one ear
   cocked for an announcement.
Then we are bused off
  to overnight accommodations,
  with food vouchers in one hand,
  luggage in another,
  and turbulent emotions in our hearts.

Patient and kindly Lord,
  I would learn patience, today.
  "All things are passing," St. Teresa said.
  When this disappointment has passed,
    let patience take root in
    me.
  Grant that I may go forward, again,
    in peace.
Amen.

Be patient, therefore, beloved, until the coming of the Lord. The farmer waits for the precious crop from the earth, being patient with it until it receives the early and the late rains. You also must be patient. Strengthen your hearts, for the coming of the Lord is near....See, the Judge is standing at the doors! As an example of suffering and patience, beloved, take the prophets who spoke in the name of the Lord.

JAMES 5: 7-10

Waiting Room

Lord,
  we are a microcosm of the universe
    in this space,
  a curious cross-section of the human family.

Fifty years ago, we were travelers in bus depots and
    in train stations.

But life changes; the perennial human aspiration
    to spread wings, to take flight,
    to defy gravity
    has led us to this airport,

    and here we wait.

Remind me that waiting
    is a basic human experience;
    it should not be squandered through
      seeking distractions offered
in the airport's boutiques;
    it should not be resented when
        time moves slowly.

Lord,
    you who are Alpha and Omega,
        the beginning and the end,
        the first and the last,
    grant me the wisdom
        and the imagination
    to know the worth of rubbing shoulders
        with these men and women in their waiting.
    If you will, bless them. I entrust us all
        to your never-failing care.
Amen.

Humble yourselves therefore under the mighty hand of God, so that he may exalt you in due time. Cast all your anxiety on him, because he cares for you. Discipline yourselves, keep alert. Like a roaring lion your adversary the devil prowls around, looking for someone to devour. Resist him, steadfast in your faith, for you know that your brothers and sisters in all the world are undergoing the same kinds of suffering.

1 PETER 5: 6-9

Close Call

Lord,
> there was one flight I nearly didn't make;
> a last minute snow flurry, a rented car,
>> a wrong turn on the *autobahn*,
> and there we were, speeding away from the airport!

> Somehow, it all worked out.
> A minivan rushed luggage and us
>> out to a plane on the runway:
> straining from Munich to Paris,
>> leaving monks and music behind.

Lord,
> long ago, you gave us the answer
>> to moments of panic and pressure:
> the single eye of the sage,
>> the simple heart of the lover,
>> with purpose, intention, awareness.

> With your cross,
> be the stillness
> at the heart of my turning world.
Amen.

When it was evening on that day, the first day of the week, and the doors of the house where the disciples had met were locked for fear of the Jews, Jesus came and stood among them and said, "Peace be with you." After he said this, he showed them his hands and his side. Then the disciples rejoiced when they saw the Lord. Jesus said to them again, "Peace be with you. As the Father has sent me, so I send you." When he had said this, he breathed on them and said to them, "Receive the Holy Spirit.

JOHN 20:19-22

The Montreal Airport
July 14, 1987

Lord,
    no one suspected this could happen:
    thunderstorms in Toronto,
    late flights out of L'Ancienne Lorette,
        in Quebec, and
    missed connections at Dorval.
    But wait! There is more.
    A torrent isolates the airport like an island,
    a body of land surrounded by water:
    arteries closed, telephone lines down,
    food supplies emptied, everyone stranded.

    Nothing to do,
    but find a corner and spend the night.
    We are all too tired
    to be anything but quiet; we are
    too frantic not to be compassionate
    to one another.

Lord,
    in the quiet and compassion,
    you are with us,
    for you pray constantly to the Father
    in the features that are ours,

and whenever two or three of us
are gathered together.
Let it be so, always.
Amen.

"*Therefore I tell you, do not worry about your life, what you will eat or what you will drink, or about your body, what you will wear. Is not life more than food, and the body more than clothing? Look at the birds of the air; they neither sow nor reap nor gather into barns, and yet your heavenly Father feeds them. Are you not of more value than they? And can any of you by worrying add a single hour to your span of life?...For it is the Gentiles who strive for all these things; and indeed your heavenly Father knows that you need all these things. But strive first for the kingdom of God and his righteousness, and all these things will be given to you as well.*"

"*So do not worry about tomorrow, for tomorrow will bring worries of its own. Today's trouble is enough for today.*"

MATTHEW 6:25-27;32-34

Prepare for Landing

Lord,
  It's time for this flight to end.
  I've been away long enough
    and far enough.

  "All things come home at eventide,
  Like birds that weary of their roaming…"

  I, too, am glad to be homeward bound.
  That doesn't mean I'm tired
    of the adventure,
    of the travel,
    of the challenge each new place brings.

  In my heart of hearts, I know
    that each day carries me closer
    to the ultimate homeward journey.

  I do not want to fear that voyage,
    Lord of life!

  I want to spring from life to life,
    from this world to another,
    from promise to fulfillment.

Lord,
    You are life,
        the truth of life,
        the way to life.
    Lead me through the present landing
        and every homeward step
    toward that home I can call my own
        forever.
Amen.

"Do not let your hearts be troubled. Believe in God, believe also in me. In my Father's house there are many dwelling places. If it were not so, would I have told you that I go to prepare a place for you? And if I go and prepare a place for you, I will come again and will take you to myself, so that where I am, there you may be also. And you know the way to the place where I am going." Thomas said to him, "Lord, we do not know where you are going. How can we know the way?" Jesus said to him, "I am the way, and the truth, and the life. No one comes to the Father except through me."

JOHN 14:1-6

GROUNDED

Lord,
> I guess I never thought,
> seriously,
> that the day would come
> when I would no longer
> be able to fly;
> all the facts are in, however,
> and I am earth-bound,
> grounded.

> The sky is filled today
> with blue and clouds
> and distant planes—
> distant Lilliputians' toys.
> But I am here,
> with a heart that longs to be
> airborne.

Lord,
> You have made us for yourself
> (Augustine knew!)
> so let our hearts be restless,
> always and everywhere,
> until we rest in you:
> in every now and in eternity.

Amen.

Therefore, since we are justified by faith, we have peace with God through our Lord Jesus Christ, through whom we have obtained access to this grace in which we stand; and we boast in our hope of sharing the glory of God. And not only that, but we also boast in our sufferings, knowing that suffering produces endurance, and endurance produces character, and character produces hope, and hope does not disappoint us, because God's love has been poured into our hearts through the Holy Spirit that has been given to us.

ROMANS 5:1-5

Daily Strength for Daily Needs
One Year of Biblical Inspiration
ISBN: 978-0-7648-0234-8

Daily Strength for Daily Needs gives readers the opportunity to experience the Bible on a daily basis. Meditations from the Bible provide uplifting information and fresh inspiration connecting readers to the diverse themes found in Scripture. It includes: a narrative that relates the Scripture to a theme on practical living; a thought for the day; and a brief quotation from a wide variety of historical and contemporary authors.

Europe's Monastery and Convent Guesthouses
A Pilgrim's Travel Guide, New Edition
ISBN: 978-0-7648-1780-9

This new edition is the single largest resource ever compiled on Europe's monastery and convent guesthouses. It is an extraordinary guidebook featuring more than 275 places of spiritual retreat in 17 countries including updated maps and information.